"Anna and the Germ That Came to Visit"

By Christianne Klein & Helene Van Sant-Klein, RN, LMFT, LPCC

For Livia . . .

ISBN: 978-0-9840132-2-7
Library of Congress Control Number: 2020906308
Layout and Design by Daniel Yeager, Nu-Images
Concept design by Dan Sattel
Illustrations by Helene Van Sant-Klein, RN, LMFT, LPCC
Edited by Hannah Skaggs

Once upon a time,

there lived a little girl named Anna.
She lived with her mommy and daddy in a peaceful
place not too far away . . .

One day, a germ came to visit.
It was so small that no one could see
it, but it was there . . .

Cough!
Cough!

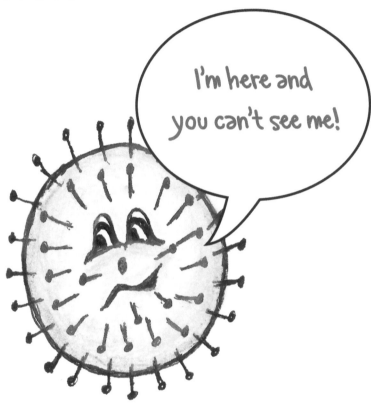

I'm here and
you can't see me!

. . . and it was making
some people sick.

Because they couldn't see the germ, it was hard for everyone to believe it was real.

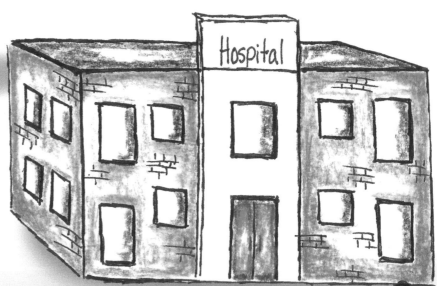

But more and more people in Anna's land were getting sick and going to the hospital. People were getting scared.

"Keep that germ away from us,"
cried the frightened citizens of the neighboring land,
and they made rules to try to stop the spread of the
germ. People weren't allowed to travel between lands.

That didn't work.
The germ was tricky.
It kept spreading and making more germs.
Soon, people realized they now had germs in their neighborhoods.

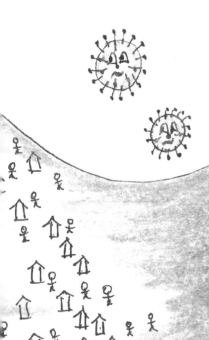

Within a few days, many lands had their own germ problems. People everywhere were getting sick.

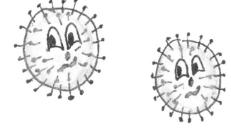

Anna and her family learned more about the germs by watching the news on TV.

One doctor on TV said, "If we stay far away from each other, the germs can't spread as fast."

"We need to wash our hands more often and clean them for at least 20 seconds every time.

We also need to stop touching our faces—especially our noses, eyes, and mouths. That should help make the germs go away," said a doctor from the neighboring land.

Anna enjoyed washing her hands. She liked how the soap and water covered her fingers with bubbles.

She learned that her favorite nursery rhyme was exactly 20 seconds long!

That made it fun to count the time as she washed her hands!

Mary had a little lamb...

People tried to stay farther away from each other, stopped touching their faces, and washed their hands.
The changes helped. Fewer people were getting sick.

But the germs were stubborn. They didn't want to leave and were still spreading.

"We need to do more! Too many people are still getting sick and our hospitals are almost full. Everyone must stay at home until the germs go away," said the mayor.

She also ordered the schools, restaurants, playgrounds, and businesses to close.

"This will give the doctors and nurses more time to take care of people who are already sick now. It will keep us from spreading more germs, too," she said.

"But how will I play with my friends if the schools are closed and we have to stay home?" asked Anna.

"You can still talk with your friends on the phone and play with your toys at home," said Anna's mommy.

"This won't last forever—just until the germs go away. After that, you can play with your friends again at school and on the playground."

"How can I give you and Daddy hugs if we have to stay away from each other?" Anna asked.

"We can still hug each other," Anna's mommy said as she squeezed her tight.

"We just can't get close to other people outside our family and house right now. We don't want to get sick and we don't want to get them sick either."

So they waited a few days inside their house. Anna did everything she was supposed to do. She washed her hands.

She talked with her friends on the phone, played with her toys, and waited for the mayor to say she could go back to school.

She wanted to go back to school most of all.

She missed her favorite teacher.

She *really* missed her friends.

Anna felt **sad** and **mad** sometimes. It was hard to understand why everything changed so fast.

Even after spending a few days inside, people were still getting sick.

"Mommy, will I get sick?" Anna asked.

Her eyes grew big.

"Or will you or Daddy get sick?!"

"Anna, you seem scared. I understand how you could feel that way. Not everyone gets sick, and most of the time, they only have a little cold," Anna's mommy said as she brushed Anna's hair.

"We're staying safe at home. Some people can get very sick from the germs. If we stay home a little while longer, everyone has a better chance of staying healthy."

Anna looked up at her mommy. "I don't want anyone to get sick, but I'm **sad** and **lonely** and **bored**. I miss my friends, and Grandma and Grandpa!"

I know, Anna. It's hard. I miss my friends and Grandma and Grandpa too," said Anna's mommy as she looked into her eyes.

"So does Daddy. We miss going to work. It's OK to feel sad or lonely sometimes. We just need to wait a little longer. **We will all get through this together.**"

Anna's mommy took her hands.

"If you are feeling scared, lonely, sad, or mad, Anna, you can talk to me anytime. You could even try to draw out your feelings."

Talking about her feelings
really helped Anna.

She also liked the idea of
putting her feelings on paper.

She sat down with her
crayons and started to draw.

**That also made
her feel better!**

Anna was happy to be with her family, but still felt confused because she didn't know when she would go back to school.

Anna's mommy said, "I know what we can do! We can think of some other things that will help us feel better. I have some good ideas, and I bet you do too."

So
...they played games together. They danced in the kitchen. She played tag in the backyard with Daddy.

They baked cookies together. They watched their favorite TV shows. They read Anna's favorite books.

Anna talked to her friends, her teachers, and Grandma and Grandpa on the phone.

She was having so much fun!

She wasn't even feeling scared about the germs anymore. She wasn't feeling lonely, sad, or mad about not being at school and missing her friends.

Then one day, just as quickly as they came, the germs were gone.

The mayor was overjoyed.

"The germs are gone! The germs are gone! No one needs to stay at home anymore! We are open for business!" she proclaimed throughout the land.

Everyone was happy!
. . . especially Anna!

"Now we can go back to work and you can go back to school and play with your friends," said Anna's mommy.

And so they did.

But they also remembered what they learned. They learned that they should still wash their hands because it helps keep other germs away. They learned how much fun it is to play together at home as a family.

They learned how helpful it is to talk about their feelings.

They also learned that if the germs ever came back, they'd know exactly what to do and they would be able to get through it . . .
together.

CPSIA information can be obtained
at www.ICGtesting.com
Printed in the USA
BVHW020607010520
579027BV00005B/476